How To Draw
HORSES

Written and Illustrated by **Carrie A. Snyder**

Watermill Press

Background

Horses originated fifty million years ago. In ancient times, people rode horses and used them to pull vehicles. In early America, horses helped pioneers settle the wilderness. They also led soldiers into battle. Today the horse has been replaced by the automobile, the "horseless carriage," as a basic means of travel. Once, the pony express was the main means of communication. Now we have the telephone. Nevertheless, we shouldn't forget the important role the horse played in our history. Horses are now mostly used for pleasure and sport. People all over the world gather to see these beautiful animals in shows and parades.

Materials

Drawing is a skill that grows with practice. It's a matter of teaching your eyes, hands, and mind to work together.

To start, you'll need some white drawing paper. The size of the paper is up to you. It's a good idea to also have some tracing paper. This will allow you to practice by tracing over the drawings in this book. But remember, you should always try drawing the horse on white drawing paper also.

An eraser is important for any artist. It's hard to get something right on the first try. A kneaded eraser is good because you can shape it and pick out highlights with it. It won't leave crumbs on your artwork like gum erasers do.

Be sure to have a #2 pencil and a 6B pencil. You can also use a black pencil for the dark horses if you like. The 6B pencil has a softer lead than the #2 pencil. It will give you darker tones. A #2 pencil is good for putting in your basic outlines. Last, but not least, you should have a can of fixative so your final drawing won't smear.

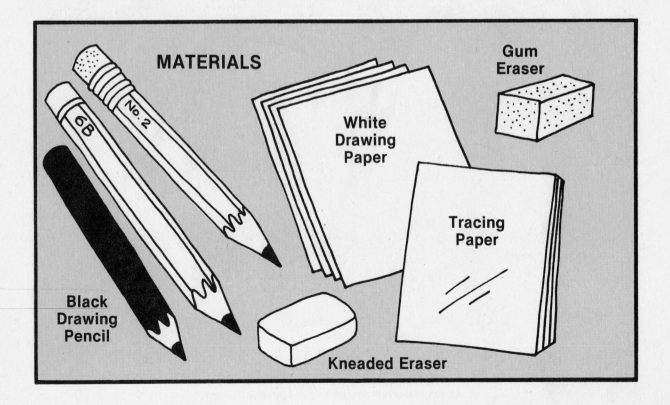

MATERIALS

6B · No. 2 · Black Drawing Pencil · White Drawing Paper · Gum Eraser · Tracing Paper · Kneaded Eraser

Technique

This page shows the different ways your pencil can be used to give different effects. For instance, to show the hair on the mane and tail, use the point of your pencil. To shade parts of the mane and tail, use the side of the point. This will allow you to cover a larger area. Some horses have smooth, thin coats, like the Thoroughbred. Others, such as the Percheron, have thick, hairy coats. The samples below tell you how to achieve these different textures. You can also see how the pencil should be used to make a finished drawing. The more you practice these techniques, the better you will get. Most important of all, have fun!

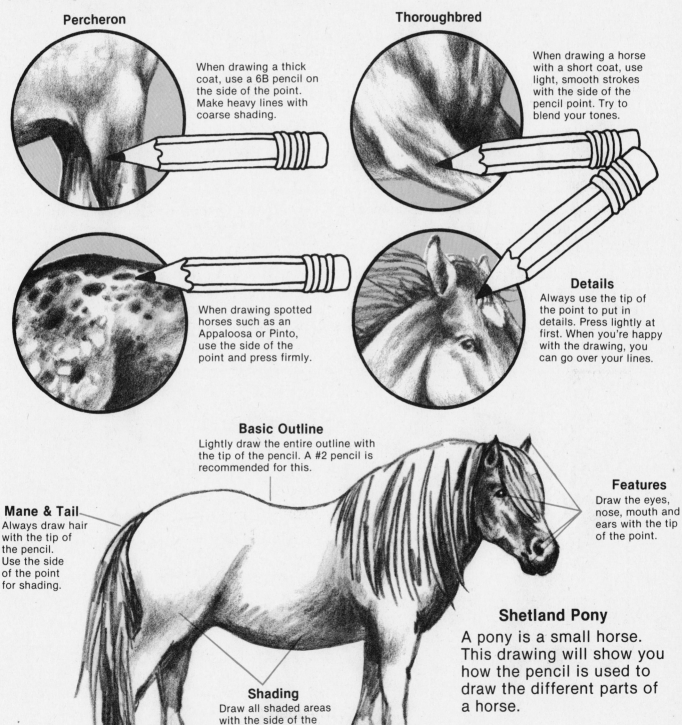

Percheron

When drawing a thick coat, use a 6B pencil on the side of the point. Make heavy lines with coarse shading.

Thoroughbred

When drawing a horse with a short coat, use light, smooth strokes with the side of the pencil point. Try to blend your tones.

When drawing spotted horses such as an Appaloosa or Pinto, use the side of the point and press firmly.

Details

Always use the tip of the point to put in details. Press lightly at first. When you're happy with the drawing, you can go over your lines.

Basic Outline

Lightly draw the entire outline with the tip of the pencil. A #2 pencil is recommended for this.

Features

Draw the eyes, nose, mouth and ears with the tip of the point.

Mane & Tail

Always draw hair with the tip of the pencil. Use the side of the point for shading.

Shetland Pony

A pony is a small horse. This drawing will show you how the pencil is used to draw the different parts of a horse.

Shading

Draw all shaded areas with the side of the point. Press lightly at first. For darker tones, press harder.

PARTS OF THE HORSE

Before you can draw any breed of horse correctly, you have to know its anatomy. Study the different parts of the horse below. This will be a big help when you draw the various horses in this book. If you leave something out, the drawing will not look right. Come back to this page if you need help.

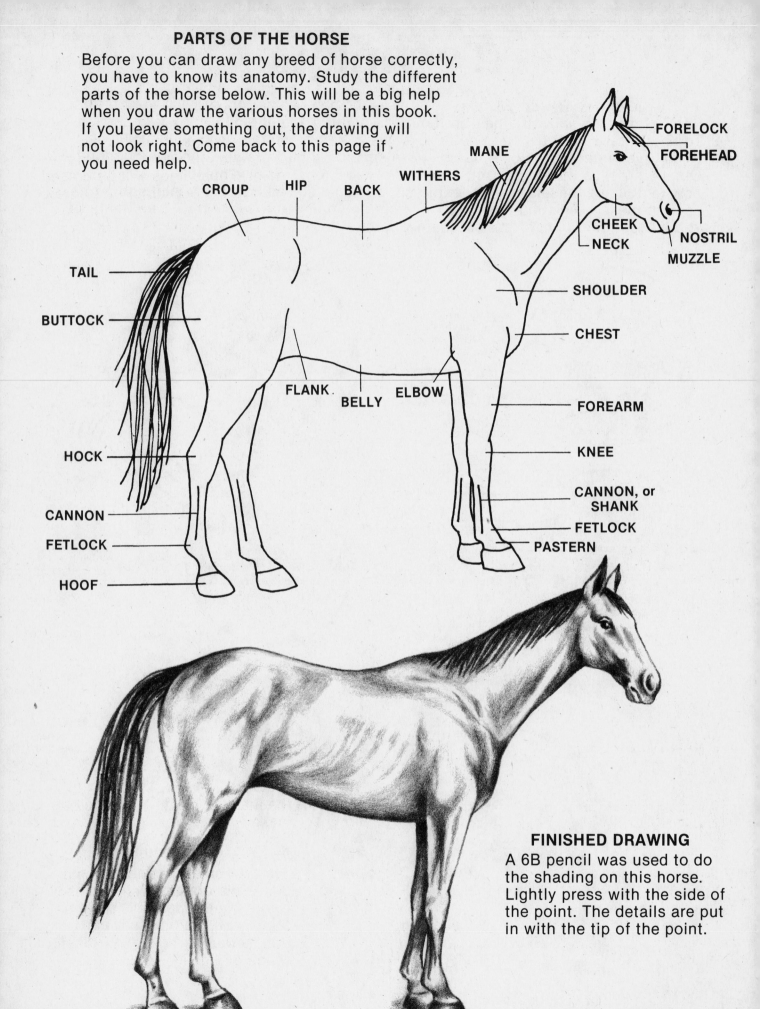

MANE

WITHERS

CROUP   HIP   BACK

FORELOCK
FOREHEAD

CHEEK
NECK

NOSTRIL
MUZZLE

TAIL

BUTTOCK

SHOULDER

CHEST

FLANK   BELLY   ELBOW

FOREARM

KNEE

HOCK

CANNON, or SHANK

FETLOCK

CANNON

FETLOCK

PASTERN

HOOF

FINISHED DRAWING

A 6B pencil was used to do the shading on this horse. Lightly press with the side of the point. The details are put in with the tip of the point.

Basic Shapes

HEAD

HINDQUARTERS

CHEST

STEP 1

Always begin your drawing with the three body masses: the head, chest, and hindquarters. A #2 pencil is good for this. Lightly press with the tip of the point. These lines will be erased later. It is good practice to draw these shapes on tracing paper over the finished line drawing shown below. After tracing these drawings, be sure to try it on your own.

STEP 2

Draw the lines for the back, neck, and stomach. Add the jaw and muzzle. Put in the eye, nostril, mouth, and ears.

STEP 3

Draw the legs and hoofs. Add the mane and tail. Now you can make your finished outline. Study the different lines that make up the horse's head. If you look carefully, you'll see a jaw and even a lower lip. When you're happy with your outline, start to put in the shading. Don't forget to erase your basic shape guidelines.

Heads

THOROUGHBRED

When drawing the head of any horse, first lightly draw in your two basic head shapes: a circle or oval for the top of the head, and a cone for the bottom. If you are drawing a front view of the head, it helps to put in a guideline for the eyes. Draw a line for the jaw. Add the eyes, nose, mouth, and ears. All your features should be drawn in lightly at first. When you are happy with them, go over the lines. Study the finished drawing and put in your finished outlines. Erase your basic shape lines before you put in the shading.

PERCHERON

3/4 VIEW
Eye protrudes.

SIDE VIEW

Remember to show the curves for the lip and chin when drawing your finished outline.

Features

The unique features of a horse are very important to the overall drawing. Take extra time to study the different features of the horse you're drawing. It would help to practice drawing them on a separate piece of paper before you draw them on your basic outline. Remember, the more practice, the better you'll get. This page shows you how to start. See if you can do the drawings shown below.

NOSES

Lightly draw the shape for the nostril, the inside of the nose. The nostril has a lip around it that you can show by drawing a curved line. Add shading to the inside of the nose and around the outside of the curved lines.

EARS

To draw a horse's ear you just have to remember two basic shapes: An upside-down "V" for the outside, and a large water-drop shape for the inside of the ear. See the sample.

LEGS

When drawing all the legs on the horses in this book, be sure to include the shapes shown below. The front legs have knees and the back legs have hocks. All legs have fetlocks and hoofs.

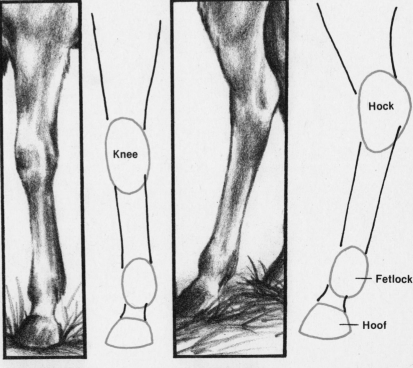

FRONT LEG

BACK LEG

EYES

Start the eye by drawing an almond shape. Put a circle in the middle, leaving a little white in each corner. Draw a line for the eyelid. Shade in the center of the eye with the side of the point of your pencil. Leave a white highlight to give the eye sparkle.

Arabian

The Arabian, or Arab horse, is the oldest purebred horse known to man. It dates back to the sixth century A.D., when it was first bred to be used on the desert.

Horse breeders all over the world use Arabians to develop new breeds, because of their great endurance. When an Arabian runs, its tail flies high in the air.
These horses come in all colors, but the most popular colors are white and dapple gray.

The Arabian has a refined head. Notice the taper on the head shown in the circle. Remember to leave a highlight in the eye.

FINISHED ART
Use the side of a 6B pencil for the shading. Press lightly, because this horse is a gray Arabian. The shading shouldn't be too dark.

TO BEGIN:

Draw your three basic body shapes. Add the lines for the neck, back, stomach, and muzzle. Draw an eye, ear, nostril, mouth, and tail. Now put in the legs and hoofs.

FINISHED LINE DRAWING

Use the tip of the pencil to put in the hairs for the mane and tail. Draw the finished outline of your horse as shown here. Erase the original guidelines. You can now start the shading. Look at the finished art on the opposite page.

American Saddle Horse

The American Saddle Horse was originally bred in Kentucky to serve as a fast, comfortable means of travel for wealthy plantation owners. This breed is known for its five gaits: the walk, trot, canter, prancing slow gait, and faster rack. A beautiful breed of horse, the Saddle Horse is a mixture of Thoroughbred and Morgan. It can be bay, brown, or chestnut in color.

Two of the most outstanding characteristics of the Saddle Horse are: the strongly arched head and neck, and the high-flying tail. This breed also lifts its legs very high in what is called a fast rack gait. The horse below illustrates this.

FINISHED ART
Study where the highlights are in this drawing. Put in your shading with the side of a 6B pencil.

Draw the three basic body shapes. Add the lines for the back, neck, stomach, and muzzle. Draw the eye, ears, nostril, mouth, and tail. Now add the legs and hoofs.

FINISHED LINE DRAWING
Draw the lines for the mane and tail with the tip of your pencil. Put in your finished outline. When you're happy with the sketch, erase the basic guidelines. You are now ready to put in your shading.

Quarter Horse

The Quarter Horse is traditionally known as the cowboy horse of the West. Cowboys still use them on ranches to herd cattle. The Quarter Horse is a mixture of the English Thoroughbred and the original Spanish horses used in North America. This horse gets its name from the one-quarter-mile races it was famous for running. Quarter Horses are fast and sure-footed, which also makes them great barrel racers in rodeos. They come in all colors.

Pay special attention to the chest muscles of this running Quarter Horse. Also note that three of the horse's hoofs are off the ground.

FINISHED ART
Use the side of a 6B pencil point to do the shading. Press lightly because the shading on this horse is not very dark. Don't forget the shadow on the ground around the right rear hoof.

Draw the three basic body shapes. Notice that on this horse, the shapes overlap in the stomach area. Add the lines for the back, stomach, neck, and muzzle. Draw the ears, eye, nostril, mouth, and tail. Notice that the ears are back in this drawing. Put in the legs and hoofs.

FINISHED LINE DRAWING

Draw the lines for the mane and tail with the tip of your pencil point. Finish your outline and erase your old guidelines. You can now put in the shading. See the finished art.

Percheron

The Percheron was originally bred in France. It gets its name from its home district in France, the Perce. The Percheron is a strong working horse. There's a trace of Arab blood in its breeding. Although it weighs over a ton, this horse is not known for eating a lot. The Percheron is a quiet-mannered, obedient horse. It's either black or gray in color.

The horse shown here is dapple gray. Study the finished art below and you will see a pattern of white spots. To achieve this pattern, shade around a small circle or oval shape, leaving the center white.

FINISHED ART
Use a 6B pencil for the shading. You can use broad strokes for the hair on the legs. This breed has a thick coat, so the shading can look a little coarse. Use the side of your pencil.

14

Lightly draw your three basic shapes. Add lines for the back, stomach, neck, and muzzle. Now draw the eye, ears, nostril, and mouth. Put in the outlines for the legs and tail. You are now ready to make your finished line drawing as shown below.

FINISHED LINE DRAWING

Study the lines of the Percheron's head in the circle on the opposite page. Now make your finished outline. Put in the hairs of the mane and tail. Add some hair to the legs. Erase your guidelines for the basic shapes. When you're happy with your outline, start shading your horse. Study the finished drawing on the opposite page.

Thoroughbred

The Thoroughbred was first bred in England from the Arabian horse. Today the Thoroughbred is bred all over the world because of its great speed and beauty. Thoroughbreds have powerful legs and make excellent racehorses. They are also used as hunters and jumpers. You'll often see them in horse shows. They come in all colors.

The head of this Thoroughbred is very expressive. Pay special attention to the mouth and nostril area. Because this horse is rearing, its basic body shapes will be located in different places than the other horses in this book. Take your time to draw them correctly.

FINISHED ART

Use the side of the point for shading. Press lightly and blend your tones. There are many highlights on the short, shiny coat of this horse. Use the tip of the point to put in the grass.

Draw your three basic shapes. In this case it would be good to use an oval for the hindquarters. Add your lines for the stomach and neck. Draw the muzzle, this time leaving a "V" shaped opening for the mouth. Put in the ears, eye, and nostril.

FINISHED LINE DRAWING

Draw the hairs for the mane and tail. Study the drawing in the circle for the details of the head. Add teeth to the open mouth. After you are happy with the finished outline, erase your basic shape guidelines. You can now start to put in your shading. Study the finished art on the opposite page. Pay special attention to the shoulder muscles.

Palomino

The Palomino is a beautiful horse with a golden coat and a blond, silky mane and tail. This horse originated in the United States. There is some question about whether the Palomino is a breed or not. It is actually a combination of many breeds. The Palomino always stands out in parades and shows. It is also used for hunting and jumping.

The head of this Palomino is refined. Be sure to draw in the protruding eye and nostril on the left side of the head shown here.

FINISHED ART

The Palomino is a light-colored horse, so don't make your shading too dark. Press lightly with the side of the point. For the darker areas, press harder until you get the tone you want.

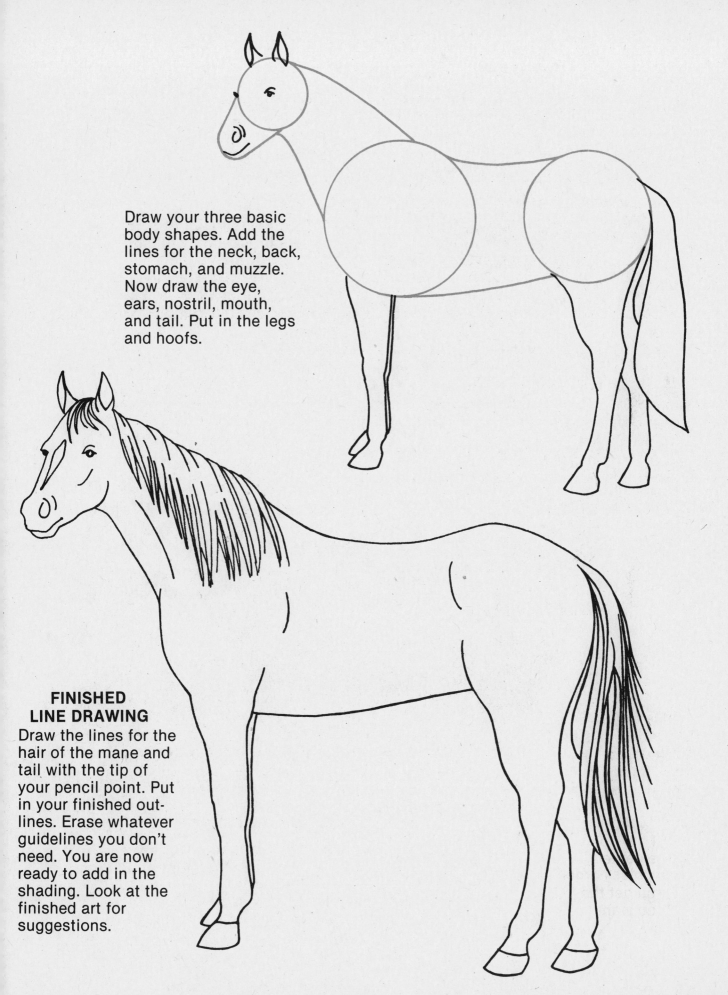

Draw your three basic body shapes. Add the lines for the neck, back, stomach, and muzzle. Now draw the eye, ears, nostril, mouth, and tail. Put in the legs and hoofs.

FINISHED LINE DRAWING

Draw the lines for the hair of the mane and tail with the tip of your pencil point. Put in your finished outlines. Erase whatever guidelines you don't need. You are now ready to add in the shading. Look at the finished art for suggestions.

Pinto

The Pinto was originally bred in the United States. A Pinto is a horse with mixed colors: black and white, or brown and white. This horse is used for riding as well as herding. Because of its unusual markings, the Pinto is often seen in parades.

Study the mane on this Pinto. Where the coat is white underneath, the hair on the manè will be white. Where the coat is black or brown underneath, the hair will also be that color. It makes the horse look very unusual.

FINISHED ART
Most of the shading is done on the spotted areas. Study the different patterns before you begin. Use the side of the point of a 6B pencil.

Draw the three body shapes. Notice the long, sloping neck on this horse. Now put in the lines for the back, stomach, neck, and muzzle. Draw the eye, ears, nostril, mouth, and tail. Put in the legs and hoofs.

FINISHED LINE DRAWING

Draw the hair for the mane and tail. When you get the finished outline the way you like it, erase your basic shape guidelines. You are now ready to put in the Pinto's spots and shading.

Morgan

All Morgans can be traced back to a Vermont-born stallion named Justin Morgan. No other horse has ever had an entire breed named after him. He was in a class by himself. The Morgan was originally used as a harness horse to pull carriages, and for harness racing. It is a solid, muscular horse. The Morgan can be brown, black, bay, or chestnut in color.

The head on the Morgan is a little shorter than most of the other breeds. This horse also has a thick, muscular neck.

FINISHED ART
This is a black Morgan: you can use a 6B pencil, or even a black drawing pencil for the shading. Since most of the shading is very dark, you'll have to press firmly with the side of the point. Leave light areas for your highlights.

Start by drawing your basic body shapes. Add the neck, back, and stomach lines. Put in the muzzle. Draw the ears, eye, mouth, nostril, and tail. Then add the legs and hoofs. You are now ready to make your final outline.

FINISHED LINE DRAWING
Draw the lines for the mane and tail. Make your finished outline. Erase your basic guidelines before you start your shading.

Foal

A newborn foal can see, hear, and—in a short time after birth—stand up and walk. Foals are all legs and are extremely awkward at first. As soon as they are able to stand up, they look for their mothers for food. A foal can't chew grass until it is two months old, so its only food is milk. After it reaches one year of age, it's no longer considered a foal. That's when the rest of its body catches up to its already long legs.

FINISHED ART
Foals have a furry coat, so you can use coarser shading lines. Use the side of the point of a 6B pencil. Add some grass for effect.

Draw your basic shapes. Notice the slope of the back. In this drawing, the hindquarters are higher than the chest. Add the lines for the back, stomach, neck, and muzzle. Since this foal is looking at you, it would help to draw a line down the middle of the head.

FINISHED LINE DRAWING

Draw the lines for the foal's short mane and tail. The mane and tail are not yet fully grown. Put in an outline for the white blaze on its head. Now draw your finished outlines. Erase all your original guidelines.

Clydesdale

The Clydesdale is one of the best-looking, and most popular of the draft breeds. This horse has long flowing hair below its knees and hocks, giving it a unique appearance. The Clydesdale is a stout, muscular horse often used for pulling wagons. A team of Clydesdales in a parade is always a favorite among spectators. Clydesdales are bay, brown, or black in color, with white feet.

The Clydesdale has a thick neck, and a long mane. This horse also has some long hairs behind its chin.

FINISHED ART
Before you start, decide where you want to leave white areas. There's a lot of shading on this horse, so press fairly hard with the side of the point of a 6B pencil.

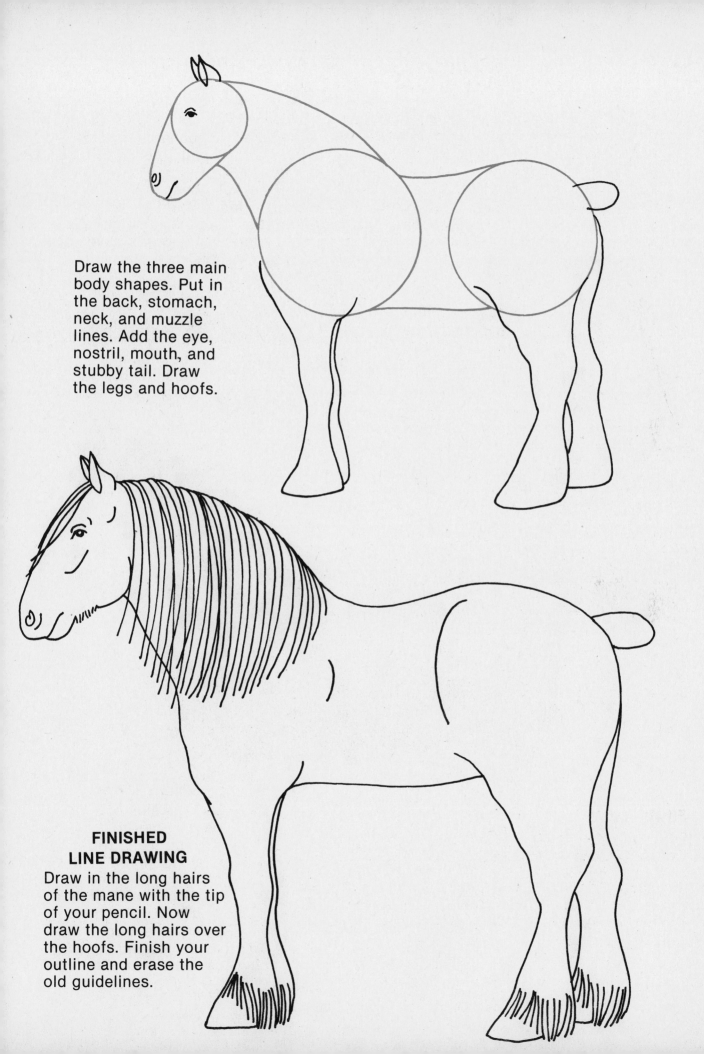

Draw the three main body shapes. Put in the back, stomach, neck, and muzzle lines. Add the eye, nostril, mouth, and stubby tail. Draw the legs and hoofs.

FINISHED LINE DRAWING

Draw in the long hairs of the mane with the tip of your pencil. Now draw the long hairs over the hoofs. Finish your outline and erase the old guidelines.

Appaloosa

The Appaloosa is a North American Indian horse with leopard-type spots. The Nez Perce Indians of Idaho and Washington originally bred the horse in the Palouse River region, where it gets its name. The Appaloosa is used as a cow pony, hunter, and jumper. It's also a favorite in the circus because of its unique markings. Appaloosas have dark brown or black spots on a roan background.

The coat of the Appaloosa is unique. Study it closely so you can capture the most outstanding characteristic of this breed.

FINISHED ART

Use the side of a 6B pencil point to put in the spots and the shading. If you look closely, you'll see that some of the spots are white. To show these, just shade around the spots, leaving the white paper showing through.

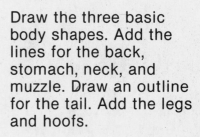

Draw the three basic body shapes. Add the lines for the back, stomach, neck, and muzzle. Draw an outline for the tail. Add the legs and hoofs.

FINISHED LINE DRAWING

Draw the hair for the mane and tail. Make your finished outline. When you are satisfied with it, erase the basic shape guidelines. Your horse won't look like an Appaloosa until you add the spots to the hindquarters.

Shetland Pony

Ponies are small horses less than 58 inches from the ground to the withers. A full-grown Shetland is only 32 to 46 inches high. It's a favorite of children all around the world. The Shetland pony originated in the Shetland Islands, north of Scotland. It was originally used to pull plows and wagons. They are usually black, brown, or chestnut in color.

This pony is short and stocky. It has a thick neck and a long mane and tail. Be sure to give it short, hairy legs.

FINISHED ART
This is a light-colored Shetland pony, so there isn't too much shading. Use the side of the point of a 6B pencil to show what shading there is.

Draw your three basic body shapes. Make a big circle for the chest area. Put in the lines for the back, stomach, neck, and muzzle. Add the ears, eye, nostril, mouth, and tail. Now draw the legs and hoofs.

FINISHED LINE ART
Draw the lines for the long hairs of the mane and tail with the tip of your pencil point. The hair covers much of the head and part of the eye. As you finish your outline, be sure to show the hair on the legs. Erase your guidelines. Now you can start to shade your pony.

Mare and Foal

This grazing mother is keeping a watchful eye on her young foal. Can you remember how to draw your basic shapes for this cute drawing? If you need help, go back to the page that tells you about basic shapes. Lightly draw all your guidelines with a pencil. If they don't look right, just erase them and try again. Don't forget, practice makes perfect. Since this drawing has two horses, it will take longer than the others. Take your time and have fun!